A Practical Guide
to
Releasing Tension
(and Increasing Energy)

A Practical Guide to Releasing Tension (and Increasing Energy)

by

Robinne Comissiona

With photographs of Natan Lev by Gili Melamed-Lev

RIVERCROSS PUBLISHING, INC. NEW YORK

ISBN: 0-944957-07-2

Library of Congress Catalog Card Number: 91-25701

Comissiona, Robinne.
   A practical guide to releasing tension (and increasing energy) / by Robinne Comissiona. — 1st ed.
      p. cm.
   Includes bibliographical references.
   ISBN 0-944957-07-2 : $10.95
   1. Stress management. I. Title.
RA785.C65 1991
155.9'042—dc20
                                      91-25701
                                          CIP

CONTENTS

FOREWORD

I came to Israel in the spring of 1959. Torn from my childhood country, Rumania, disoriented, frightened by the future, anxious to "make it" as a dancer and choreographer, I was angry and suspicious all the time. My feelings and emotions were stuck somewhere in my stomach building toward an ulcer. My short legs seemed even shorter and my whole body impossibly stiff. I was longing to be accepted by my peers and eager to do what was fashionable among dancers. Taking Feldenkrais lessons was the thing to do. I attended a Feldenkrais session and became an instant Feldenkrais "addict." The benefits were quickly evident: my body became more elongated, pain in my neck and lower back disappeared, I slept better. I felt more confident and less tense.

I worked with Moshe Feldenkrais on and off from 1959 until not long before he died in the summer of 1984. During those years he not only enlarged my horizon, he became the most influential figure in my life and work.

Inspired by his genius, I continue to look for new dimensions that can improve the quality of life.

I don't believe practicing the methods developed by Feldenkrais, Alexander, Carola Spead, Yoga, etc. will increase your longevity to a biblical one, but you will experience an increase in alertness, youthfulness and awareness until late in life.

As more and more people have become aware of the stress in their lives and the damage caused by that stress, countless methods have been developed to provide relief from stress and, in so doing, avoid the damage to body and mind.

I studied the classical ones and the modern ones, the scientific and the esoteric, the kinesthetic and the psychological. After many years I chose a few and developed them. A large part of the synthesis of my work is contained in the exercises described in this book. Even if you are a skeptic, practice them with full commitment and concentration. You will soon come to accept the wisdom of the biblical saying: "If I am not for myself, who will be for me?"

INTRODUCTION

There was a warning of heavy floods. A religious man sat in his garden and prayed. Neighbors were leaving; some asked him to leave with them. The man refused, saying God would save him.

The floods grew deeper and his garden was *seriously* flooded. A helicopter came, descended nearby and the pilot offered to help the man who was in great danger. But our man refused again, saying he had faith in God, and God would not let him perish. The waters grew deeper and deeper, and another helicopter came to rescue him. Again the man refused with the same answer: "God will save me." When the water was to his neck, a third helicopter offered help. In vain. Our man was still waiting for God to help him. Finally, the waters covered the man, he was taken by the floods and died. When in heaven, he went straight to God asking, "God, how could you forsake me when I always prayed to you, so fervently?" And God replied, "I did not forsake you, I sent you three helicopters!"

I wonder how many helicopters we miss. We still disregard the warnings against smoking, drugs and most of all—stress.

I had a very dear friend, named Hannah. She did not go out in the evening; she was afraid of being mugged. At home, she always made sure all the doors were locked and the security alarm on. She was afraid of burglars. Hannah smoked a lot, particularly during the long evenings. She died young. Hannah invited the killer into her home—it was the cigarette.

We disregard countless "helicopters" because we are too busy, too tired, or too tense to do something to reduce stress. It seems that it is even convenient to use stress as a scapegoat. We can blame stress for everything that goes wrong—mentally, physically, socially, politically, scientifically, even metaphysically.

Yet pilot rescuers are abundant. There were and there are a great number of researchers, doctors, psychotherapists, educators and practitioners whose hands are extended to you. They agree on the strong connection between mental stress, anxiety and muscular tension and muscular tension and breathing.

Wilhelm Reich, a pioneer in the concept of holistic health, emphasized that anxiety and relaxation are incompatible. Some of his principles—"only you, yourself, can be your liberator" or "you tell me what you are by way of your expression"—were once considered revolutionary. Now, because a great number of disciples were inspired to continue and develop the new path, they are revolutionary no longer.

Among the best-known techniques are: "Progressive Relaxation," developed in the United States by Dr. Edmund Jacobson; "Autogenic," completed by the German, Dr. J.H. Schultz; "Bionergetics" by Alexander Lowen and the "Quieting Response" by Dr. Charles Stroeber. Other methods which treat tension as the base of other problems, are Fritz Pearl's "Gestalt Therapy," and Dr. Milton Ericson's "Hypnosis."

Releasing tension is the "bonus" Alexander and Feldenkrais provide. Purely physical techniques like Shiatsu, accupressure or Rolfing are to be considered for their "side effect" on relaxation.

". . . bad eyes are not a pure physical problem, but the result of accumulated tension," wrote Aldous Huxley about Dr. William Bates's theory and exercises for the eyes. Meditation, yoga, reiki, magnetism are only a few of many techniques currently making inroads on the western mentality.

The fact that so many "helicopters" are flying low and so many hands are stretched to help is a warning that we are in danger.

Headaches, pains in the neck, lower back pain, many lung, stomach, heart and liver problems, unjustified anger, aggressiveness, and depression can be prevented or treated at their inception by different methods which release tension and reduce stress. I do not claim that releasing tension will cure a bleeding ulcer, a deteriorating heart or a kidney disorder. Medical doctors should treat patients; yet when medical treatment is complemented by relaxation techniques, the results are often better, faster and last longer.

Preventing stress from engulfing you will allow you to avoid disasters. "It is better to avoid the fire, than have to struggle to extinguish it."

A Practical Guide
to
Releasing Tension
(and Increasing Energy)

WHY IS THIS MORNING DIFFERENT? FEEL FOR YOURSELF!

Once Ben Gurion spoke in Hebrew to an emigrant who had been living in Israel for several years. When the Israeli citizen apologized for not speaking Hebrew, Ben Gurion commented, "Are you not ashamed for not learning to speak Hebrew after so many years?" The settler answered, "It is so much easier to be ashamed."

Are you one of those people who, believing it is easier not to do anything, struggle with tension, anxiety, and lack of energy—even apathy? Are you satisfied with the way you look? Do you believe nothing can be done to improve the quality of your life? Do you disregard all the choices offered to improve your well-being? If so, you are missing the best of life: the enjoyment of living!

Merely to talk or read about release of tension is not enough. Only practicing some of the techniques and exercises described in this book can help alleviate—or better, help you *avoid*—the dangerous effects of accumulated tension.

To experience a better day you have to begin while still in bed. Do not feel guilty for spending a few minutes practicing, while a very busy schedule awaits you. Give yourself the most precious gift we have—kindness to yourself. You deserve it!

If you learn to love yourself as you love your neighbor, not only will you benefit from the changes, but your family, friends, and colleagues will appreciate your more pleasant, patient, and relaxed attitude.

When my husband wakes up in the morning, he is energetic, impatient, and very demanding. I am a slow riser. I open one eye and take a while to start functioning. Both extreme reactions are quite common; so are those of fear, anxiety, laziness, indolence, and impatience. Of course, the weather has a great influence; when the sun is shining it is easier to start the day than when darkness keeps our eyelids closed. But whether the day is shiny or rainy, the impatient and the indolent, the slow and the fast riser will all benefit from practicing the following exercises which help to get rid of physical and mental morning stiffness. I don't pretend "copyrights" but I am not a thief either, just a collector, and I share with you the best of my collection.

With your first morning breath try to increase your awareness. Pay attention to how your body feels and the way it changes. These few easy morning exercises are more beneficial than mindless strong movements. When you start the day "fighting" your body, that antagonizing mentality will be with you for the rest of the day. By releasing tension and improving your breathing, you unlock your awareness and you are free to use it! With your awareness you can give meaning to, and enjoy *all* your activities, no matter how minor they may be.

I once took a course to improve awareness. One of the exercises was to take five minutes to eat a raisin. It was amazing how much I discovered about that raisin's texture, shape, smell, and taste. Indeed, that simple exercise made me realize how much we miss by not paying enough attention to what we do.

Awareness is one of life's most precious gifts. Start to increase your awareness by becoming aware of yourself and the people in your life. You will improve your relations with the people around you and with the whole world, physically and metaphysically.

NOW YOU ARE READY

1. Read the instructions for each exercise once before you try it.
2. Repeat each exercise at least twice before moving on to a new one.
3. Keep in mind that *how* you do the exercises is more important than how many *times* you repeat them.
4. You may shorten the exercises by repeating them two or three times or you may repeat them as many times as you like.

STR . . . E . . . TCH

1. Empty your bladder. Get back in bed and lie down on your back. Open your mouth very wide and slowly exhale. When you think you have reached the end of your exhalation, close your mouth and exhale a last bit of the air through your nose then inhale deeply. Most probably you will need to yawn. Carola Speads, in her book, *Breathing: The ABC's*, emphasizes the benefits of "intelligent yawning." Yawn fully with a wide open mouth and don't cut the yawn short.

Enjoy the increased energy that comes from stretching the lungs and giving your body more oxygen.

The following exercise, recommended also in Yoga techniques, does more than increase circulation. Its instant effects in countless situations will convince you to practice it. In the morning it will help get you started with balanced energy. During the day, it will help you when you feel sluggish, tired or bored, when you cannot concentrate, and when your mind wanders during a conversation. This exercise also counteracts the negative effects of jet lag. Try it also during the night when you have a cramp or your legs twitch. Practiced in the morning on an empty stomach it helps many people get rid of chronic constipation. It is a secret weapon with which you can combat "the facts of life":

2. **concentrate on the muscles of the anus and rectum. Then slowly contract them as deeply as you can starting with the anus and moving up toward the intestine. Do not force the contraction. Do it as slowly and smoothly as you can. Try not to involve the buttocks or abdomen! Hold each contraction for 3 to 5 seconds counting one- and, two- and, three- and, etc., and release. Rest for 2 seconds then repeat the contraction and rest. Repeat the whole set five to seven times. You may do this exercise any time, in any position: lying down, sitting, standing, walking, even while jogging.**

If you do only one or two exercises faithfully for the rest of your life, this could be one of them.

3. **Still in bed, lie on your back without your pillow. Extend the legs comfortably apart.**

Be sure your head is aligned with your spine, and is not turned or tilted. Gently press your lower back into the mattress, which hopefully is not too soft. Imagine that you have a long tail attached to your tailbone and someone is pulling it up through your legs toward your forehead; at the same time bring your chin to the chest. Let the bed support your weight. Hold this position for the count of 4. Then release for the count of 4. Release and repeat 4 times.

Be aware of your increased flexibility.

4. Still lying in bed, interlace your fingers and place your hands behind the base of your head so that you feel the skull bones in your hands. Your elbows are open to the sides. See Figure #1. Now very gently, without tensing the hands or arms and with much loving care, you are going to stretch your neck and spine. Open your mouth and slowly exhale. At the same time imagine that someone is pulling the top of your head away from your body and very subtly with the help of your hands lengthen your nape. Count to 5 and feel the nape of your neck and your spine lengthen. Then, still keeping your hands under your head, release and inhale through your nose. Repeat this exercise six times. Concentrate on how the whole spine is lengthening more and more with each repetition.

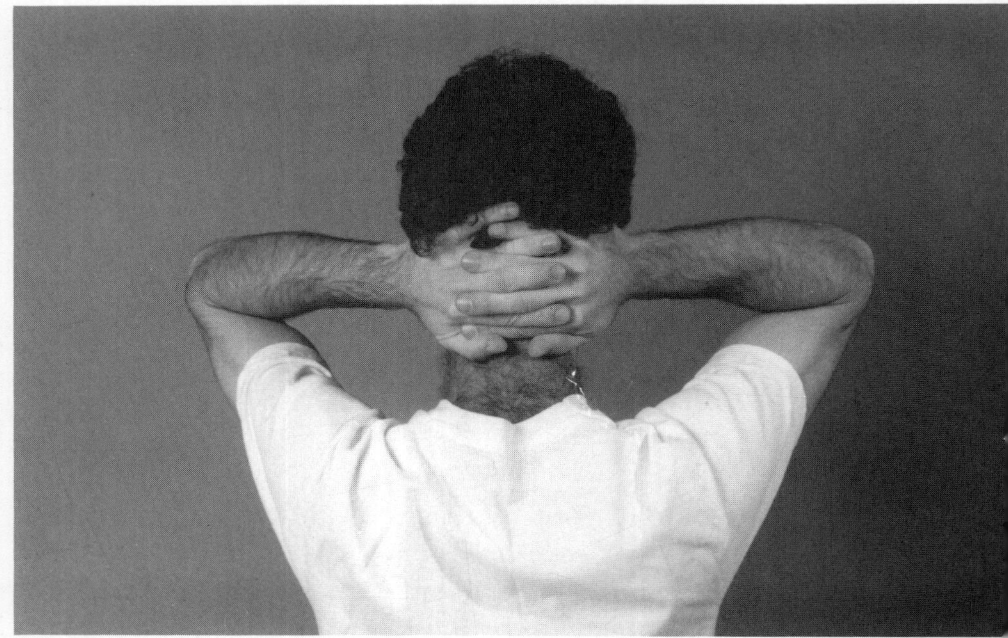

Figure #1.

"Widen your back" is an Alexander principle: Feldenrais developed some of the most efficient exercises to improve breathing through widening the back:

5. **Roll over on your right side keeping your knees slightly bent. Extend arms to shoulder level in front of you on the bed. Keep elbows locked. Place the left palm on top of the right one. See Figure #2. Keeping the left elbow extended, lengthen the left arm in front of you by sliding the right palm away from the left one, see Figure #3. Return arms and hands to their starting positions. Repeat the movement ten times. Concentrate on the changes in your body. If you pay attention, the movement becomes more interesting to practice. You**

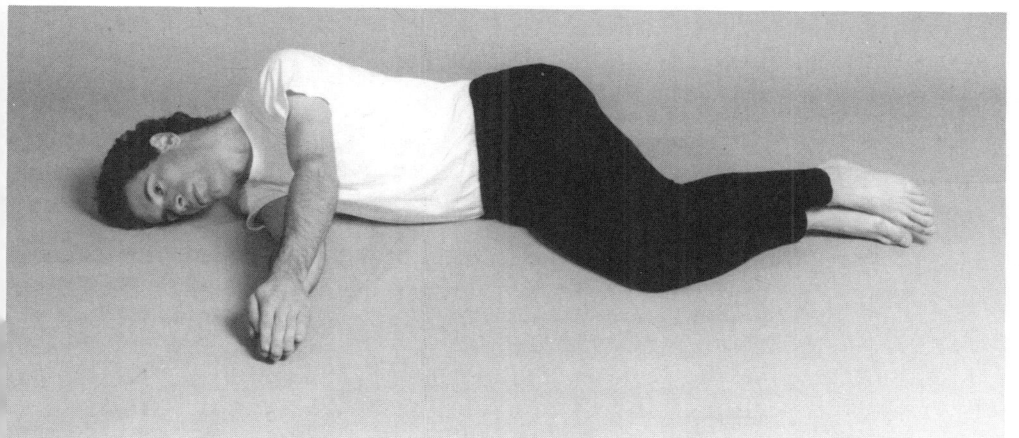

Figure #2.

will notice how the first movement starts only from the shoulder joint and with each repetition progresses toward the shoulder blade, upper spine, and lower spine.

This group of exercises will not only help you *stand* taller, it will help you *feel* taller—and stronger!

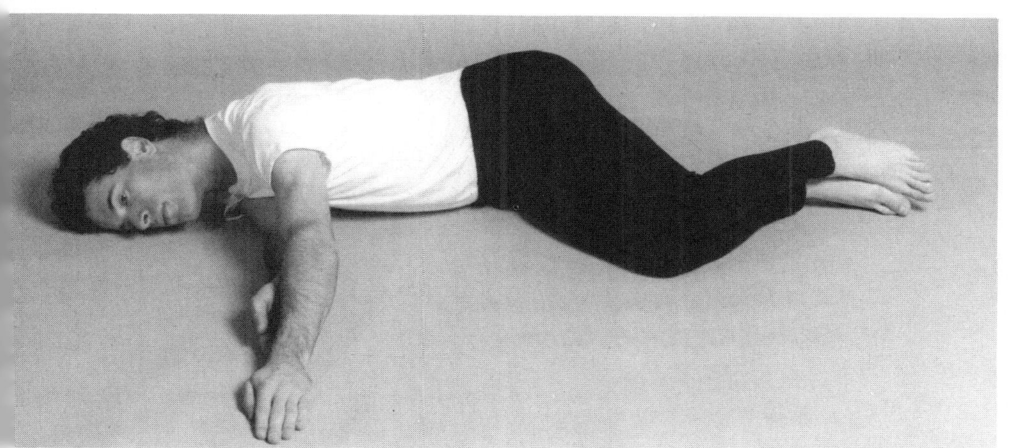

Figure #3.

Now, still keeping the elbows extended, shorten the right arm by rolling your left shoulder toward your back and return to the position you started, palms toghether. See Figure #4. Repeat the exercise about 8 times.

Combine the two previous movements. Slide the hand forward and let your chest roll a little forward and slide the arm back along the right arm and roll towards the back, repeat smoothly the lengthening and shortening of the right arm; let the chest and head participate.

Turn on your left side, bend the knees and repeat the three sequences—a) lengthen the arm forward, b) shorten it *rolling* towards the back and, 3) combine them.

Turn on your back and breath freely and I would love to hear your remarks! I assure you that you will have a welcome side effect: Your posture will improve.

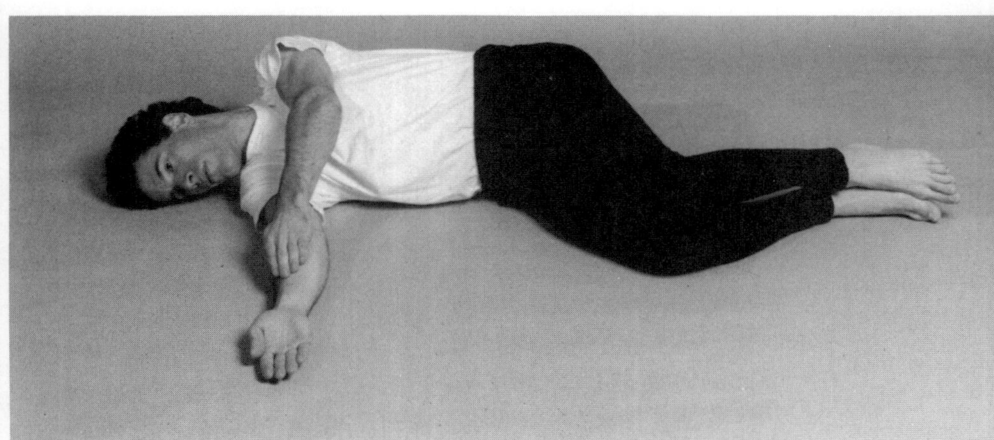

Figure #4.

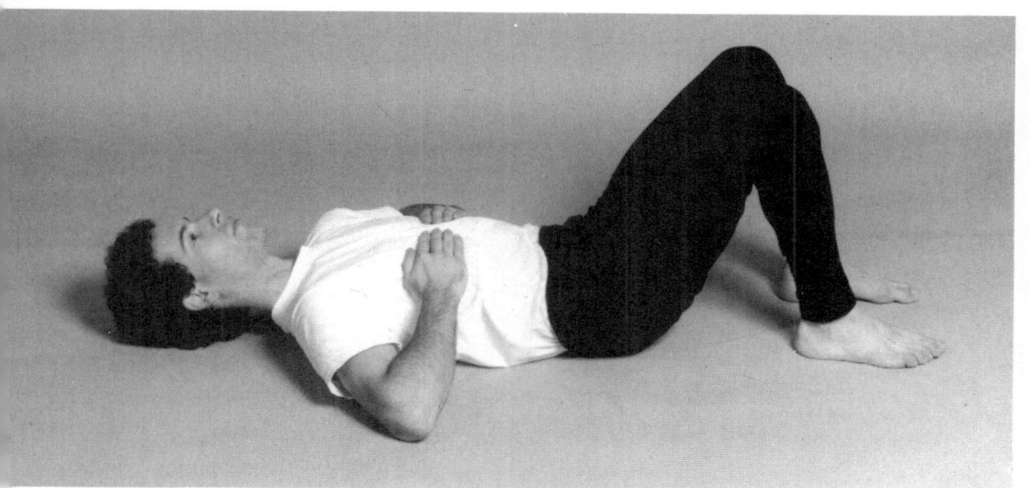

Figure #5.

6. Lie on your back knees bent, feet comfortably apart. Place your hands on both sides of your lower ribs, elbows extended. See Figure #5. Take a deep breath. As you slowly exhale press your hands into your ribs. Then, keeping your wrists in place, raise your elbows slightly. Release the pressure and inhale. Repeat 4 times.

Concentrate on the way your back muscles expand and contract. Enjoy their new flexibility!

7. Still on your back, extend your legs. Place your arms alongside your body, palms down. See Figure #6. Flex the right foot by directing the toes towards your knees. Push your right heel away from you toward the end of your bed. You will feel the movement in your hip joint. Relax both feet and flex the left foot. This time push your left heel away from you toward

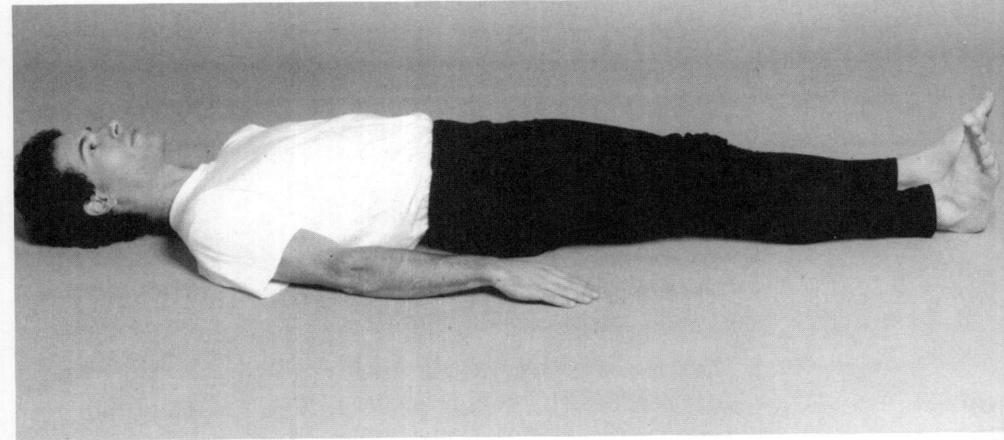

Figure #6.

the end of the bed. Repeat each movement slowly 3 times alternating the feet. Gradually increase the speed but always give yourself time to feel the stretch in your hip joint.

Your walk will benefit greatly from this exercise.

8. Sit on the edge of the bed, feet flat on the floor hands on your thighs. See Figure #7. *Keep looking straight ahead* as you slowly turn your head from side to side. Do this 5 or 6 times. This movement can be repeated during the day. It considerably eases the neck muscles.

Why are these exercises different from others you may have heard or read about? The uniqueness of these exercises is the gentleness with which you treat your body. There are no jolts to the bone or muscle; there is no jumping or bouncing. Be gentle with yourself, and be aware of the changes your body is feeling.

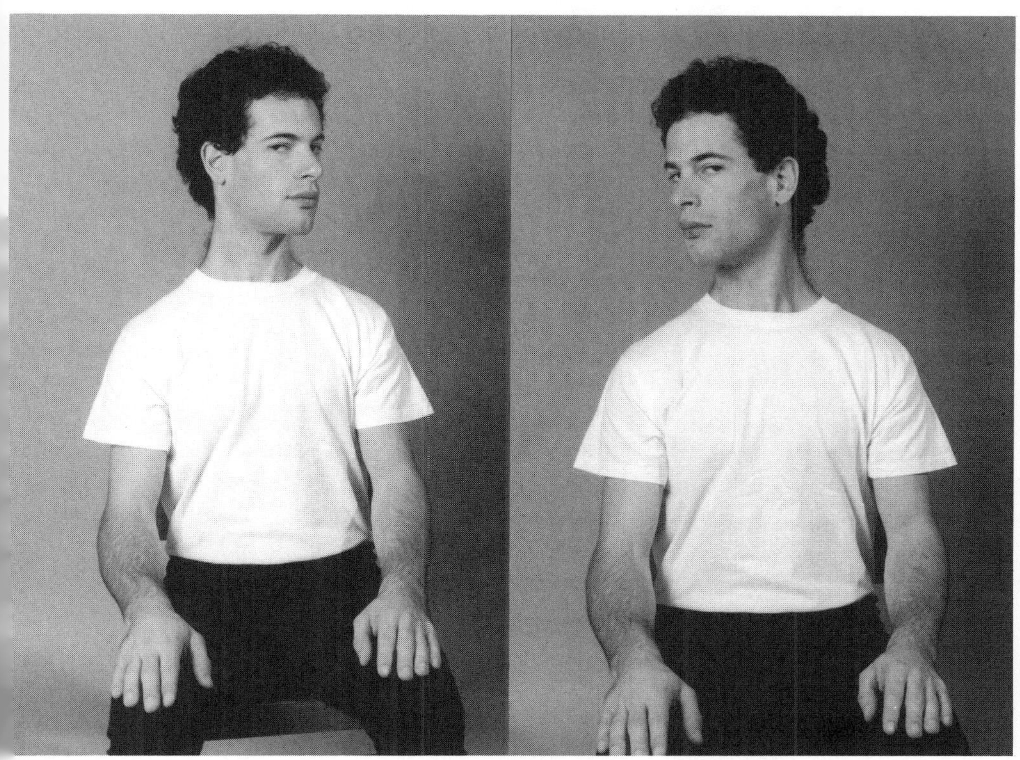

Figure #7.

Think of these exercises as a gift you are giving yourself every day of your life—a gift of energy, flexibility, and the healthy, attractive appearance people respond to. Then ask yourself—who deserves this gift more than I?

VISUALIZE TO COMBAT ANXIETY

Spend a few minutes and imagine—step by step—the way you would like to act and react to what you consider "frightening encounters" of the day: a staff meeting, an audition, a job interview, a discussion with fellow employees and/or members of your family.

Don't lose time and energy building your anger. Rather, imagine you are an actor on a big movie screen. Picture the situation that is making you nervous. Now imagine yourself acting in a positive way in that situation. If you want to imitate an ideal hero or esteemed friend, do it. Go through this imaginary rehearsal with full awareness.

I can't promise you *la vie en rose*, but the grey moments will become more colorful. You cannot control all the situations you have to face during the day, but you can learn to control your reactions. Unimportant problems which sometimes assume gigantic, menacing shapes will be reduced to their minimal importance. You will feel better and will be able to stand up under pressure.

Do not expect your life to change. The baby will cry, your spouse or child will be argumentative, your boss will sometimes be unpleasant; inflation will rise, international political conflicts will be unsettled; water and air will continue to be polluted and so on. But YOU will change. You will see beyond life's dark moments, you will be able to see and cope with the full range of life's joys and sorrows.

FACING THE BOSS

You always want to perform your best for your boss. But suddenly, just before a job review or staff meeting, you begin to panic and lose confidence. As well prepared as you are, you suffer from memory loss and are haunted by past failures. Even if you aren't a "believer," you implore God to help you, "just this one time." You become shy and confused. Your mouth is dry and you feel nauseated. At times you may find yourself angry, jealous, or over-confident.

In this chapter, I recommend some "instant" tools to improve your power of concentration and memory, tools that will make you look and act your best. They will also help you avoid a dry mouth, lapses in memory, and even nausea. Remember, these are "emergency" techniques to use when time is limited.

This section describes a variety of "savers" that will protect and rescue you instantly. The benefits are short-term, but guaranteed!!

In spite of our desire to look confident, breathing betrays our nervousness. The average breathing rate—about 15-18 cycles per minute—under tension becomes much quicker and more shallow. There are many ways to improve breathing. Here is a very efficient one.

BREATHING TO RELAX

Just before "facing the boss" slightly part your lips and exhale slowly and steadily pronouncing an endless quiet "SSSSSS." Then breathe deeply. Repeat two or three times. Any boss will prefer to deal with a relaxed, happy-looking person.

Anxiety and insecurity worsen our appearance when posture mirrors our feelings.

We recall our mothers' and teachers' "Stand straight!" As a result we stiffen our body, breathe even faster, look rigid, and less attractive.

To improve posture, which should be a balanced one, I recommend the following:

> **If seated, sit evenly on both buttocks. Keep your feet flat on the floor. Do not cross your legs.**
> **If standing, be sure your weight is equally distributed on both feet which are slightly apart.**
> **As you inhale imagine you are pulling your breath up from the base of your spine along the inside of your spine to the top of your head. As you exhale imagine you are exhaling through the crown of your head. Visualizing your breathing in this way will gently lengthen the spine. When you repeat this experience, pay attention to the way your neck is lengthening.**

The above is a key exercise to reduce tension in any situation and the first step in all breathing remedies. When your posture is well-balanced and upright, you are more alert and your thinking is clearer.

BANISH MEMORY LAPSE

One theory concerning the brain states that by increasing the physical awareness of the brain, you improve its functions:

I have had spectacular results in cases of memory lapse. Linda, an advanced voice student, although very well prepared for her final exam, could not remember certain foreign words. After practicing the following exercise, she remembered the forgotten words and successfully passed her exam.

Close your eyes and visualize your brain. Then, as you gently inhale, visualize the air going into your skull. Now imagine the air slowly circling two or three times around your brain at eye level. Part your lips and exhale slowly for as long as possible. Repeat, changing the direction of the circles. Remain calm and relaxed. The words or names you forgot will pop back into your mind. Guaranteed!

Long ago I experienced a similar practice during a Jean Houston workshop. It was always successful.

BREATHING TO STIMULATE THE BRAIN

More and more research is revealing that the brain's right side is the center of creativity while the left side controls rational behavior. Alternative nostril breathing, a yoga technique, stimulates both sides of the brain, improving balance and awareness, as well as clarity and creativity. It is an instant activator, but should be practiced in privacy before going to "face the boss."

Sit comfortably. Place the middle finger of your right hand in the middle of your forehead. The right thumb closes the right nostril. Inhale through the left nostril. With your ring finger, close the left nostril and release the thumb. Exhale through the right nostril. Keep the right nostril open and inhale

through it. Close the right nostril with the thumb and release the right ring finger, exhaling through the left nostril. Continue the cycle 3-5 times. You will feel stimulated and energized.

NO MORE DRY MOUTH

Just when you want to have clear speech and perfect diction, does your mouth get so dry you cannot make a sound? Here is a solution.

With the index finger, press and release the spot below and behind the ear between the lower jaw and neck. See Figure #8. If your mouth is still dry, gently explore that area until the saliva rescues you. Once you discover the "magical" point, you can practice unnoticed whenever you need to.

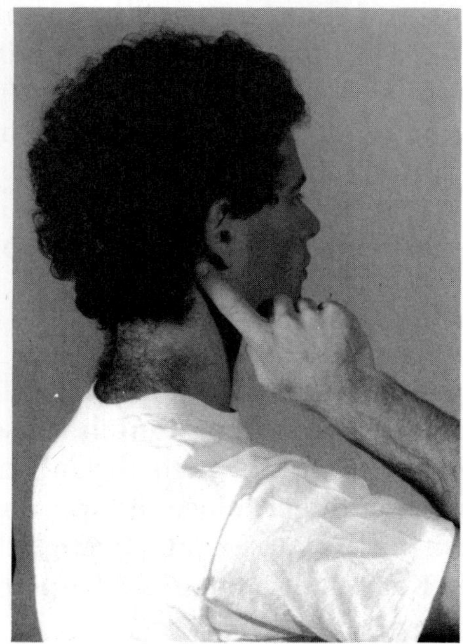

Figure #8.

By the way, saliva contains some hormones which help keep you young.

FIND YOUR LOST VOICE

It may have happened to you during a job interview or speech. You open your mouth and you sound like a mouse! Your words are squeaky and shaky. Your voice quality tells everyone that you are nervous. To be sure your voice will not fail you, I recommend combining the therapeutic healing power of your own hands with the following autosuggestive techniques:

Figure #9.

Rub your hands until they feel warm. Place them around the front of your neck with the heels of the palms meeting in the middle and the fingers embracing the sides of the neck. See Figure #9. Breathe in while whispering "I am." Hold your breath and say, "Calm." Part your lips, exhale slowly for as long as possible, repeating the words "relax" and "confident." Repeat the entire experience for at least a minute.

RELAX YOUR JAW

If you grind your teeth or have a tight jaw because of tension, try this exercise.

Place the fingers under the temple in front of the ear. Open and close your mouth

Figure #10.

20

and feel the jaw hinge. Place the heels of the palms on both sides of the jaw joints. See Figure #10. Press and slide the lower jaw away from the upper one. Your mouth will slowly open as there are no muscles supporting the jaw and mouth. Place the back of your right palm under your chin and press up the lower jaw until the lower teeth barely touch the upper ones. See Figure #11.

Figure #11.

STOP NAUSEA

Do you ever feel nauseated when you are nervous? Although many western doctors resist eastern techniques, the following technique is recommended by some physicians for combatting nausea caused by tension.

Press the fleshy part of your left hand with the index finger and thumb of your right hand. See Figure #12. Press and release 20-25 times on each hand.

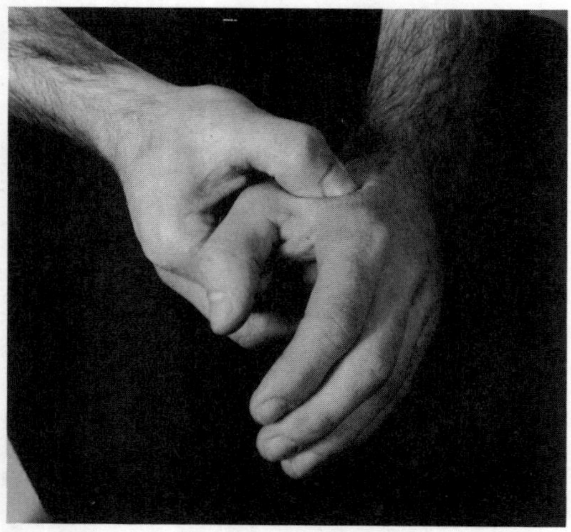

Figure #12.

SMILE, SMILE, SMILE

It is said that our eyes are the "windows" of emotional stress. Just when we want to look pleasant, friendly and warm, a frozen smile and fixed eyes spoils our appearance and shatters our confidence. It has been proven that when you smile at your plants and pets, they grow stronger and healthier. A sincere smile has a warming and energizing effect and increases the activity of the thymus gland. Here is a Taoist thought about smiling I would like to share with you. "Living with an inner smile is to live longer, in harmony with yourself."

Let's practice the inner smile!

Close your eyes. Inhale. As you exhale, slightly part your lips and without any mouth movement or facial expression, think and feel that you are smiling with your eyes. With the next exhalation, feel the warmth of a deep inner smile on your forehead. With the third exhalation, direct the smile to your mouth. Remember, do not move your mouth or change your facial expression. Voluntarily, if time permits, smile inwardly with the entire face. Open your eyes. Look in the mirror. You will project warmth, love and confidence.

Although you may not work on a stage, you are a performer. Whether at school, at work, or at home, you seek approval and recognition on "life's stage." I would like to underline one of Dr. Hans Selye's principles and stress that our tension grows from our imagined need to act as someone we are not.

If you practice these exercises, you will be ready to act spontaneously, yet exercise the control you need, and experience deep awareness and enjoyment.

FACING THE PUBLIC

Neck, shoulder and lower back pain.
A racing heart.
Cold hands.
Tremors.
Constant worry over a disturbing thought.
Insomnia.

These are just some of the physical and psychological costs you pay for being a performer.

There is no doubt that tension is a creative and essential ingredient in a performer's life. It is a delicious, stimulating spice. You must have a certain amount of it to be successful. But when tension becomes overwhelming, it becomes harmful.

As a young performer, you aren't aware of the mental and physical price you pay for success, but as you grow older, your ability to cope with tension diminishes. Poor health and emotional imbalance slowly affect your life. "Escapes" like smoking, drinking, or drugs provide only temporary relief and themselves create more problems.

You shouldn't necessarily avoid tension; you must be able to control it.

Recently, a celebrated pianist who proudly admits she practices at least 7-8 hours a day played magnificently one of the most demanding piano concerti; during the monumental work she missed only one note. The triumph was overwhelming, the public was exuberant, the musicians effusive with praise, so was the conductor; but the pianist felt and looked miserable. All she could think about was the missing note. She left the concert hall without wanting to see anybody. Indeed her attitude was so negative some people began to wonder if they had really heard an outstanding performance.

The way we react depends so much on the degree of tension we live with. In this case the pianist was so strained that the smallest unnoticed error assumed giant proportions and ruined the memory of a splendid concert.

Nothing is more infuriating, frustrating and depressing than when after rehearsing non-stop for hours and hours, instead of improving, things get worse.

Short breaks to release the accumulated tension will help improve your performance and increase your power of concentration.

TAP TO RELAX

Tapping is one of the key remedies against tension. It is an old akido technique but Carola Speads deserves the credit for the successful way she systematized it. In her New York apartment-studio overlooking Central Park hundreds of people—performers and non-performers—learn to tap themselves, tap each other, and live happily ever after.

It is a "pick-me-up" technique. Use it in many situations as a coffee substitute but do not practice it before going to bed; it will keep you awake.

With your hand slightly cupped, tap your rib cage all over, starting from the base of the neck and moving to the shoulder joint. Next, go to the front of the rib cage and continue as far as you can reach over the shoulder to the back. Then tap along the sides of the rib cage from the armpit to the last rib.

Tap three times at each spot. Make sure you cover the entire rib cage with the exception of the breast and pit of the stomach. Tap the right side with your left hand and the left side with your right hand.

To see instant results, tap only one half of the rib cage. I suggest tapping the right side with the left hand first because it is usually more tense. Stop after 2-3 minutes of tapping and feel how much more alive your right side is. Check your breathing! Look in the mirror! Do you see that your right shoulder is lower? The right side of your face should have a more relaxed expression and your sight should be improved in the right eye. Now repeat the tapping treatment on the other side.

With your renewed energy, visualize the difficult passage, scene or dance steps you were practicing. You will be surprised to find how easily you remember and perform them.

THE ONE-MINUTE STRETCH

I suggest tapping plus an extra one-minute exercise for pianists and string players.

1. Sit comfortably with your legs apart and both feet on the floor. Your right hand rests on your right thigh, your left hand on your left thigh. Palms are faced down and fingers extended. To achieve correct posture, slightly part your lips and inhale and exhale slowly. As you inhale, imag-

ine you are pulling the air up along the side of the spine into your skull. Then imagine you are exhaling it out through the crown of your head.

2. Now slide the right hand down the leg keeping your elbow straight. Slide it as far as it will go without straining. See Figure #13. Do not bend the body, the movement should come only from the shoulders. Keep the hand in contact with the leg and return to the original position. Each time you slide your hand down the leg, exhale through slightly parted lips.

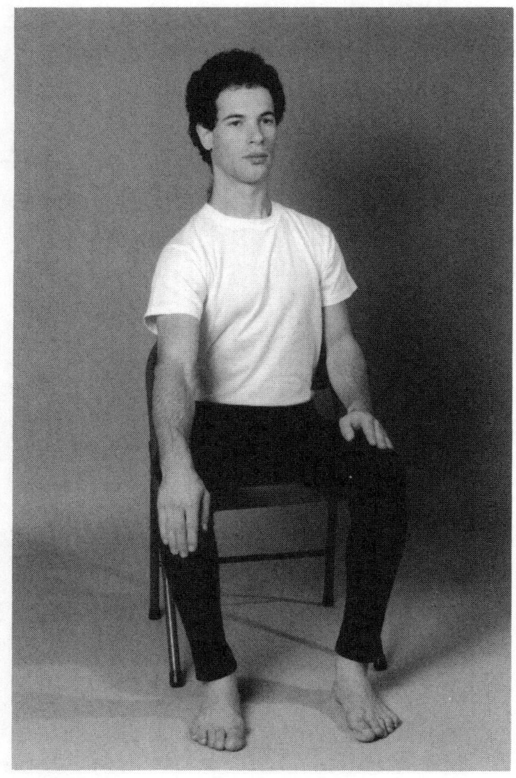

Figure #13.

When you return to the original position, inhale through your nose. Repeat this sliding movement 10-15 times and then rest for a few seconds.

3. Again slide the hand along the leg, but this time, bend forward from the hips, keeping a straight back and the head in line with the spine. You will have the feeling that the crown of your head is leading the forward movement. See Figure #14. When you return to the initial position, check the head to see if it is balanced on top of the spine, almost as if it were hang-

Figure #14.

ing from the ceiling, not forced forward or backwards. Each time you slide your hand down your leg, exhale through slightly parted lips. When you return to the original position, inhale through your nose. Repeat this movement 10-15 times.

To check the results of this experience, extend both arms in front of you, shoulder height. Notice how much longer the right arm has become. Walk around the room and pay attention to how much more relaxed and alert your right side feels. Repeat the set of exercises on the left side of your body.

So that tension does not accumulate, you should do this one-minute exercise after every hour of intense rehearsing.

Just before going on stage, even on stage when conditions permit, you will instantly feel calmer and in control if you apply the following control breathing technique:

With your mouth puckered and slightly open, exhale just a drop of air, as if you were blowing into a straw; release the lips and hold. With the puckered mouth, exhale another drop, pause, and breathe out, alternating exhaling and pausing until you exhale the last drop of air. Close your mouth and inhale through your nose. Imagine the air travelling down into your abdomen. You will feel the improvement after one round but 3-4 rounds will have a more therapeutic effect.

"EYEING" TENSION

Many practitioners assert that if you release the tension from your eyes, you release one quarter of the accumulated body tension.

The "I Can't Sleep" chapter contains a full, very efficient, complete eye treatment. But for a mini-fast improvement, when you are studying a score or a script and you feel your eyes tiring, try this:

Rub your palms until they are warm. Close your eyes and place your hands over your eyes. The heels of the palms cover the

Figure #15.

31

eyes, fingers cover the forehead. See Figure #15. Visualize darkness on your imaginary mental screen. Concentrate on being "bathed" in velvet black color. After 1-2 minutes, remove your hands. Slowly open your eyes and check the score or script's print. Do you see more clearly?

HEAR STRESS DISAPPEAR

Relax your ears! When the muscles around the ears are tense, not only is your hearing affected, but also your balance. Using your finger tips, press and release the bone behind and below the ear. Continue to press and release along the sides of the neck until you reach the collar bone.

LETTING GO

When you are enraged—your partner received more flowers or applause, or the reviewer was unfair—do not add more fuel to the fire. Release your tension and get rid of wicked thoughts by trying the following:

Cross your wrists one wrist over the other using the heels of your palms, press and release along the breastbone. See Figure #16. Starting from the top, travel down inch by inch as far as you can feel the bone. Do not press on the pit of the stomach. As you press, exhale with a long "FFFFF." Inhale when you release the pressure.

Figure #16.

MEDITATE

To quiet the mind, to expand energy and increase sensitivity, nothing works better for a performer than meditation, the ultimate art of self control and discipline.

There is nothing strange or occult about the technique. In his books, the *Relaxation Response* and *Beyond the Relaxation Response*, Dr. Herbert Benson scientifically proves the physical benefits of meditation. Please experience and evaluate for yourself.

The basic technique is simple. The meditator silently repeats a certain word or sound for 10 to 15 minutes, twice a day. Do not pay attention to interfering thoughts. Do not fight them. Let them come. Let them go.

At the Beth Israel Hospital in Boston, the following form of meditation is recommended:

Select a one- or two-syllable word or sound like "one." I have had good results with people choosing their favorite word, or the name of a loved one, "God," "Lord," "peace," "shalom," etc.

Assume a comfortable sitting or lying position. Close your eyes. Breathe slowly. With every exhalation, silently repeat your word for 10-15 minutes.

At the end of your time open your eyes and remain where you are for a minute or two. Then get up.

If the thought of "having" to meditate twice a day is anguishing, you will not be "punished" if you occasionally only practice once a day, or even only occasionally. The real motivation to meditate regularly will come from within yourself. It will result from the way you feel and act after meditation.

One of the basic rules of "orthodox" meditation is never to fall asleep during meditation. I am not so strict. If you are silently repeating a word, a sound or a phrase from a prayer and you fall asleep, do not feel guilty. Enjoy the full benefits of your catnap. You will feel rested for the rest of the day.

For performers, I suggest that you choose a very short musical phrase or theme. Silently repeat it for 10 minutes in a quiet environment. Let the breath take its own rhythm. If you include a 10-minute meditation as part of your pre-performance ritual, you will experience a clear mind and increased sensitivity.

Another experience similar to meditation will help to ease tension that is centered in your stomach. It is based on the power of your hand/touch.

Rub your hands until they become warm. Then place them on the pit of your stomach. Your fingers should be extended with no space between them. See Figure #17. It is at this point that a network of nerves and

Figure #17.

fibers form the solar plexus. Close your eyes. Visualize the sun shining and sending its warm rays to that spot. Breathe silently through your nose for about six counts out, three counts in. Repeat 2-3 minutes.

STAND TALL

When standing on stage, your anxiety and lack of confidence can affect your posture. When this occurs, imagine your tailbone pulling your spine down behind your heels while the crown of your head pulls your spine up, up, and up.

RELEASE CRAMPS

During a performance or rehearsal, and while you are walking or sleeping, you may get a cramp in your hands, arms, legs or feet. If so, contract the anus, not the buttocks, as deep as you can for about 10 seconds and release. The cramp will be gone in less than 10 contractions.

EXHALE STRESS

When you are on stage and the "eyes of the world are upon you," the easiest way to regain control is to slightly part your lips and exhale a deep, long and very soft "FFFFFFF."

VISUALIZING SUCCESS

Still some more advice to be included in your mental preparations, at home or just before your performance. Close your eyes and visualize. Imagine all the sequences and aspects of your performance. Imagine every small detail, imagine the best and be prepared for the worst. Imagine the hall filled to capacity; imagine only ten people in the audience. Visualize all the situations. Do not think learning a part or a score is all you have to do. You must also mentally rehearse your actions and reactions, from the moment you step on stage to face the public, to how you acknowledge the applause and leave the stage. When you are on stage, every "unimportant" detail is magnified by the audience's eager eyes. You should look like you are acting spontaneously, but be well in control.

Margot Fonteyn, "the" English ballet star, knew well how to nourish the public's enthusiasm after her performance. She always followed the same ritual. She took a flower from the bouquet she just received, kissed the flower and offered it to her partner. Although she performed the same "act" after every performance, it always looked totally spontaneous.

And some backstage advice. Just before going onstage, trust and believe with all your being that the public who came loves and admires you. And so it will be!

OH! I AM SO TIRED!! BLAME IT ON BREATHING

"What a day! I'm exhausted" is often the answer to the evening's "How are you?" Sometimes you feel totally exhausted when you did not do any work. To be bored is as exhausting as being overworked.

Fatigue in general, and mental exhaustion in particular, are the results of poor blood oxygenation. The brain—which weighs about 3 percent of the body weight—consumes 25 percent of its oxygen. Poor breathing is the main cause of insufficient blood oxygenation. There is a strong relation between muscular tension and restricted breathing; between poor posture—slouched or rigid—and loss of energy. It is impossible to improve the quality of breathing without releasing the muscular tension. It is not an overestimation to say that the diaphragm movements may be the body's most important. During the breathing process it moves up and down like a piston. The bigger the diaphragm movements the healthier the body. When exhaling, the higher it goes, the more residual air is eliminated. When inhaling, the lower it goes, the more the lower part of the lungs will be filled with fresh air. In addition, the diaphragm massages the abdominal organs—particularly the liver and spleen—stimulating their functions. Also the brain movements are synchronized with the breathing. The brain contracts with every inhalation and expands with every exhalation. Under tension, the diaphragm, which is a muscle, loses its flexibility; its movements are greatly reduced. This in turn may cause many sicknesses.

When the diaphragm is not relaxed the whole effort of practicing breathing exercises is disappointing. I have watched many "breathing lessons" which have had more damaging effects than therapeutic ones, when the zealous student tensed the shoulders as well as the jaw, the tongue, the throat, the face, the eyes and, of course, the diaphragm. Indeed one of the most common mistakes is to protrude and draw in the abdomen by force.

In this chapter, I will recommend a number of stimulating breathing exercises, some of them borrowed and reshaped from yoga. I cannot emphasize enough the importance of complementing them with other relaxation tools like lengthening the spine or tapping the chest. The chapter "Preventive Treatment" provides most of the "release of tension" movements. All the following "energizers" should be done at less than full capacity, keeping in mind that you are not competing with anybody, and that in this circumstance less is better.

All the countings are just suggestions, not rules. Adapt them to your personal ability and enjoy the natural improvement.

BEGIN WITH GOOD POSTURE

The spine should always be well balanced and straight because it plays a key role in the accomplishment of breathing stimuli. Always begin with the "exercise for better posture":

1. **Part your lips and exhale.**
2. **Inhale through the nose and concentrate. Imagine that you are inhaling at the base of the spine and with your mind power, pulling up the breath from the tailbone up along the inside of your spine to the**

top of your head.

3. **As you exhale, imagine that you are exhaling through the crown of your head.**

SMELL GOOD, BETTER, BEST

The following advice is an "overture" that will increase your sense of smell and enhance your breathing:

> **Inhale through the nose and imagine you are directing the air toward the top of the nasal cavity between the eyes. Exhale freely. To check the improvement, smell something—a flower, a perfume, a spice—in your usual casual way. Then smell the same thing again, this time directing the air toward the upper passage between the eyes. You will be surprised how much you have increased your sense of smell.**

TO HOLD, OR NOT TO HOLD

There are different opinions about holding the breath—after inhalation with full lungs, or after exhalation with empty lungs. Actually the lungs are never completely empty. Even with the best exhalation only about a sixth part of residual air is exhaled.

While holding the breath is beneficial, it can be dangerous for people with high blood pressure. Consequently, I recommend holding the breath no longer than 2-3 seconds between and during each breathing cycle. Not all breathing exercises include the holding periods.

When you are not "in the mood" to do anything, the following exercise will help you feel good:

1. **Through slightly parted lips, exhale slowly. When you think you have exhaled all your air, close your mouth and exhale an extra drop of air through your nose. Then place your relaxed, flat tongue on the upper palate and inhale slowly through your nose.**
2. **Lower the tongue, slightly part the lips and exhale through the mouth. Repeat the whole exercise about 8 times. More than likely, every breath will be a bit longer than the previous one. Placing the tongue on the upper palate during inhalation creates a certain vibration which activates the parasympathetic nervous system.**

CREATE ENERGY THROUGH DEEP BREATHING

Here is an example of deep breathing. The principle is to exhale twice as long as you inhale, in a progressive and regressive way, and hold between each inhalation and exhalation.

Please adjust the counting according to your ability:

1. **Exhale for 6 counts**
2. **Hold and pause for 2 counts without breathing**
3. **Inhale for 3 counts and hold for 2 counts**
4. **Exhale for 8 counts**

5. Hold for 2 counts
6. Inhale for 4 counts
7. Hold for 2 counts
8. Exhale for 10 counts
9. Hold for 2 counts
10. Inhale for 5 counts
11. Hold for 2 counts
12. Exhale for 12 counts, etc., etc., for as long as you feel comfortable.

After you reach the maximum—which will always improve after a few days of practicing—do the same controlled breathing in reverse. Let's say you reached 20 counts for exhalation, hold for 2, 10 counts of inhalation, hold 2, now regress.

Exhale 18, hold 2

Inhale 9, hold 2

Exhale 16, hold 2

Inhale 8, hold 2, etc., etc., until you have reached the same counting as at the beginning of the exercise. In doing the long exhalation, if you find you don't have air left before finishing the exhalation counting, just STOP and breath normally. Please keep in mind that these are exercises and not the way to breathe every day. If overused, they can have a damaging effect.

After completing one set of the previous exercises, you will feel invigorated. After the second you will probably be very energized. After the third exhausted. Don't overdo! Mix and match your comfortable pace.

ENERGIZE WITH YOUR ABDOMEN

When we laugh vigorously we contract the lower abdominal muscles. The same muscles should activate the next "energizer."

With one finger keep one nostril closed; through the other nostril exhale in a series of short, slightly forceful exhalations which start from the lower abdomen. Do not release the abdomen between each short, staccato exhalation. Be aware that with each exhalation the abdomen wall is closer to the lower spine.

When you feel the lungs "empty," inhale through the same nostril. Imagine you are drawing the air into the lower abdomen which will naturally expand. Repeat the cycle 5 times, then rest for a few seconds. Then practice the same technique through the other nostril. For the "grand finale": breathe out of both nostrils in a series of small sharp, exhalations, like gently blowing your nose, starting from the lower abdomen. With every "blow" the abdomen gets closer to the spine. When you feel you have exhaled all your air, take a deep breath through the nose.

GET YOUR BLOOD FLOWING

A very powerful way to activate the blood circulation is by contracting the anus. The following is an introductory exercise: Contract the anus for 3 counts and release it for 3 counts, breathe freely. When you tense the anus be aware of the muscles inside the rectum—the sphincters. They should be contracted as deeply as possible. Neither the buttock muscles nor any other muscles should be involved.

Although the above mini-exercise is quite beneficial, you might like to practice a more advanced version using fragmented inhalations. The following is one of many:

> **Seated, with the spine comfortably erect, inhale through the nose for 2 counts. While holding your breath, contract the anus for 2 counts. Then release the anus, for 2 counts and inhale for another 2 counts. Again hold, tense and release the anus. Inhale for 2 counts. Without exhaling, continue the fragmented inhalation as long as it is comfortable, then part your lips and exhale slowly and calmly.**

Here is another even stronger circulation activator:

> **After a good exhalation through the nose, inhale until you feel your lungs filled to their capacity. Hold and simultaneously contract the anus and swallow. Then release and exhale. You can practice this one even when you wait in the traffic, for the red light to change.**

All the previous breathing stimuli can be practiced seated, so you can make use of them anywhere, anytime, except after a heavy meal.

Keep in mind they are treatments and not the natural way to breathe.

DO AND DO NOT, TO IMPROVE YOUR BREATHING

Do practice exercises in small doses, but quite frequently.

Do them only as long as it is comfortable.

Do them when you feel "low."

Do them when you are tired.

Do them when you need to ease your tension.

Do only one sort of exercise each time.

Do the same "chosen" exercise for some consecutive days.

Do *NOT* overdo until you feel uncomfortable.

Do *NOT* mix them in the same session.

You will soon be aware of an improved sense of well-being.

After you master all the techniques explained above, and you know your reaction to them, you can use different stimuli on different occasions; during the same day, but *not* at the same time.

Do *NOT* wait until emotion and/or physical fatigue wears you out. Fight it before it overcomes you.

BE KIND TO YOUR LOWER BACK

Sitting for a long time is a stress on the lower back and a source of lower back pain. The following very subtle movement should be practiced often to keep the lower back flexible:

Select a chair with a firm seat. Sit down on both sitting bones, knees bent, feet flat on the floor, shoulder width apart. Round your lower back—pubis toward the chin—and release. When you release, allow

**the lower back to arch slightly. Repeat this
rolling of the pelvis 6-8 times. The movement
is barely perceptible, so it can be practiced
anywhere.**

The following movement is even more beneficial, but more noticeable so you may want to do it in
private. This should not stop you from enjoying its
great results. It stretches first the cervical vertebraes
and then the whole spine, stimulating the nervous
centers.

1. **Sit in the position described above. Then
   interlace the fingers and place the hands
   behind the base of the head. The palms
   gently support the head. See Figure #18.
   The entire movement should be done
   slowly and carefully.**
2. **As you exhale, lower the chin onto your
   chest while bringing the elbows toward
   each other.**
3. **Inhale while you recover the initial position, with head erect and elbows to the
   side.**
4. **While you repeat the lowering of the chin
   toward the chest, direct the forehead toward the knees. You will feel the stretching of the nape and with every repetition
   the stretching of the spine lower and
   lower.**

People suffering from hyper-thyroid should
not practice the above stretching, as it can activate the
gland.

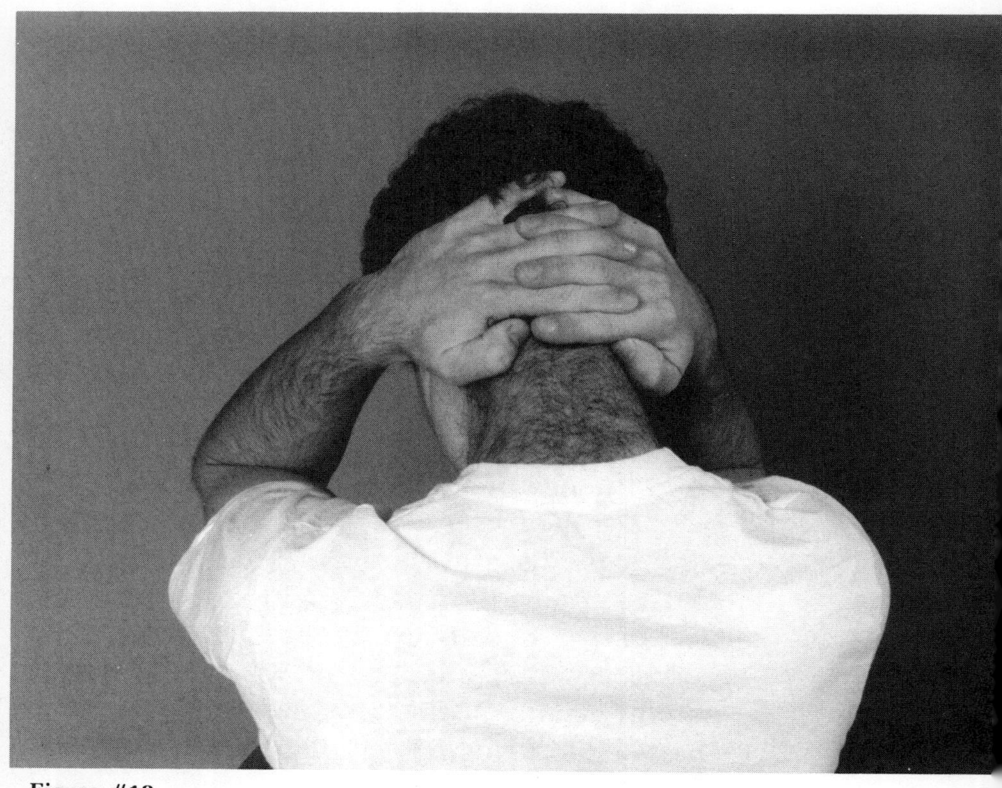

Figure #18.

TAP AWAY FATIGUE

When you feel mentally tired, use your finger tips to tap all over your head. Finish by massaging the temples clockwise and counterclockwise.

A guaranteed tool for a quick recovery is the "Tapping of the Ribcage." It is an old akido technique updated very successfully by Carola Speads. I mention it in other chapters, too, because it is a winner in many situations. It releases tension in the chest, and improves the breathing and the circulation:

48

With your hand slightly cupped, fingers together, tap all over the ribcage—except the breast and the stomach pit. Tap the left side with the right hand and vice versa.

A PINCH OF ENERGY

Like tapping, the following technique can be very useful:

Grasp the skin at your waist line with your fingers. Starting from both sides of the stomach pit, move inch by inch from the center to the sides. Never grasp the skin in front of the stomach. As you grasp inhale. As you release exhale.

A QUICK ENERGIZING WINNER

**With the thumb of one hand, press the center of the palm of the other hand and release. For variation, press and massage the palm in a circular motion and release.
With the thumb and the index, rub the lower part of the earlobe. Some 120 pressure points are located over the ear. See Figure #19.**

The rubbing of the earlobe is particularly useful immediately after meals, because it improves digestion and activates blood circulation.

Figure #19.

NEED TO CALM DOWN?

Wrap one hand and fingers around the other hand's ring finger; press and massage the whole ring finger for a few seconds. Then change to the other side.

In a few seconds, you will forget how upset you are. Try this when your boss gets you crazy!

Although recreation is not the same as relaxation, a walk, a fitness class, a bridge game, a change in your activities, can help.

By practicing these techniques one by one, you will find out which ones work the best for you.

Are you still reluctant to spend a few minutes when you are so busy and so tired? I urge you to take time out during the day to practice, the results will change your life.

If you enjoy the power of renewed energy for just one day, you will want that power every day. Give that gift to yourself. You deserve it!

PREVENTIVE TREATMENT

"THE PROOF IS IN THE PUDDING"

To prevent the damages of excessive accumulated tension, I updated a session of "Awareness Through Movements" based largely on the teachings of Moshe Feldenkrais. Moshe Feldenkrais, founder of the methods "Functional Integration" and "Awareness Through Movements," had many sides. Sometimes he was very pleasant, at other times he was extremely cynical. Sometimes it seemed as if he enjoyed embarrassing his students. I often wondered if it was part of his psychological approach to break down a student's ego in order to build a more balanced one. Whatever his "strategy" was, it definitely worked!

Today many of his movements have been adopted by therapists, health instructors, physical educators, physio-therapists, et al. Sometimes those movements are taught the way he meant them to be; they have also been adapted, adjusted, improved, and, sometimes misunderstood.

It is more than 35 years since Feldenkrais spread his knowledge. Today his theories are less revolutionary, but they are as effective as ever! One of his principles is to lengthen habitually contracted muscles; the physical changes also have great psychological effects. By doing his exercises you will not only look better, you will feel better—much better.

"Less is more" is the essence of the following group of exercises. Every movement should be done with the awareness that the joy of movement comes from inside, as well as from the improvement you will feel.

In a Feldenkrais session no rhythm is imposed, no loud music plays, there is no noise. It is a non-competitive experience and nobody is wrong. The movement is usually verbally described, to make the brain "register" and understand before translating it to the muscles. By not mechanically imitating the instructor, as is done in most exercise classes—and having to think to understand the movement, students use brain cells which might otherwise become dormant.

You can practice these exercises any time of the day or evening, but never on a full stomach. Dress comfortably and don't wear anything which can restrict your blood circulation or the freedom of breathing.

LESS IS MORE

1. **Lie down on your back on a carpeted floor, blanket, or big towel. Extend your arms along your body, palms down. Check how tense your muscles feel. Pay attention to the way your body makes contact with the floor, so you can enjoy the improvements.**

When you are very tense, your muscles are contracted and shortened and the surface of your body which makes contact with the floor is very uneven with some exaggerated arches, particularly the lower back region, hips, knees, wrists, etc. When you relax your tense muscles and "let go," you will feel your body make contact with the floor, you will let the floor support you, and you will feel the many arches flatten.

2. Let the floor support your entire body. Now slowly turn your head from side to side. Let your head be supported by the floor. Pay attention to how free or restricted or even painful the movement of the head and neck is.

3. Press the head down on the floor, hold for the count of 3 and release. Find a point on the ceiling above your head. Keeping your eyes on that point turn your head from right to left and from left to right. Practice this movement 8 to 10 times. Relax.

4. Again roll the head from side to side, this time allowing your eyes to follow your head. Do this 8 times. Rest.

5. Open your mouth wide and exhale for as long as you can. Now close your mouth and through the nose exhale an extra "drop" of air; then inhale through the nose as deeply as you can. For the next few seconds breathe normally.

6. Close your eyes. Roll your head from side to side. Be aware of how flexible your neck has become. Rest for a few seconds.

For the rest of the session we shall work mostly with the right side, so that by comparing the right and left sides the results will be clearer to your mind and to your eyes.

7. Lie down. Place your arms along your sides, palms down. Keeping the soles of your feet on the floor, bend your knees. The distance between the knees should be slightly wider than shoulder width. See

figure #20. We shall call and refer to this position as "neutral."

Gently let the right knee lean to the left, toward the floor between the legs. The right foot will naturally roll to its inside. After the right knee—without forcing—has reached your comfortable limit in approaching the floor, return the knee to the "neutral" position.

Repeat the movement eight to ten times, keeping it gentle, smooth and comfortable.

Although it looks as if the knee does the work, the hip joint is the real beneficiary of this stretching exercise.

Extend both legs, rest for a few moments, and feel the difference between the right and left sides of your body.

8.   **Bend your knees and return to the "neutral" position. Let the right knee lean to the left again, as in the previous exercise;**

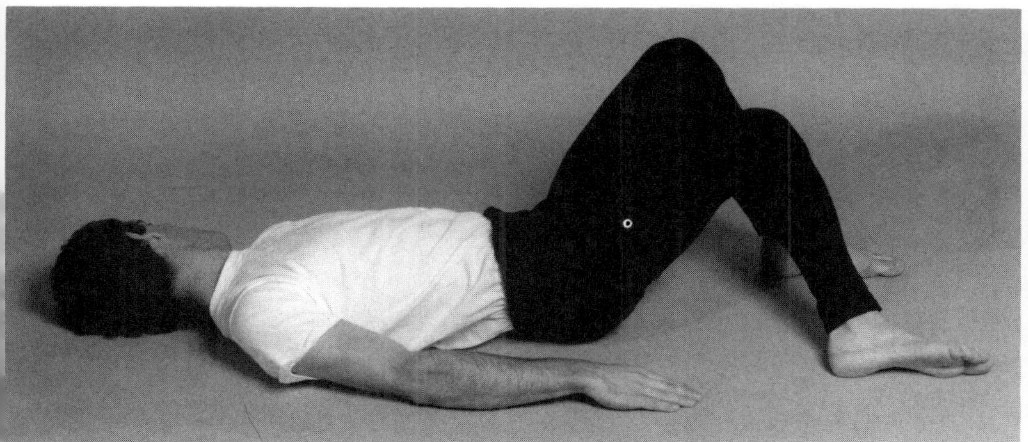

Figure #21.

at the same time, roll the head (keeping it on the floor) to the left. See Figure #21. Return both knee and head to "neutral." Do this movement eight to ten times; then extend the legs and rest for a few seconds.

9. Return to the "neutral" position with the knees bent. Again, let the right knee go to the left, allowing the right foot to roll toward its instep, but this time roll the head to the right. See Figure #22. Then very smoothly return the head and knee to "neutral." Repeat eight to ten times; then extend the legs and rest.

10. Assume the "neutral" position. Look up and fix your eyes on a point on the ceiling. Again let the right knee lean to the left. Roll the head to the right at the same time, as in the previous movement, but this time keep your eyes glued to that spot on the ceiling while you roll your head. Your right knee goes to the left, your head goes to the right, and your

57

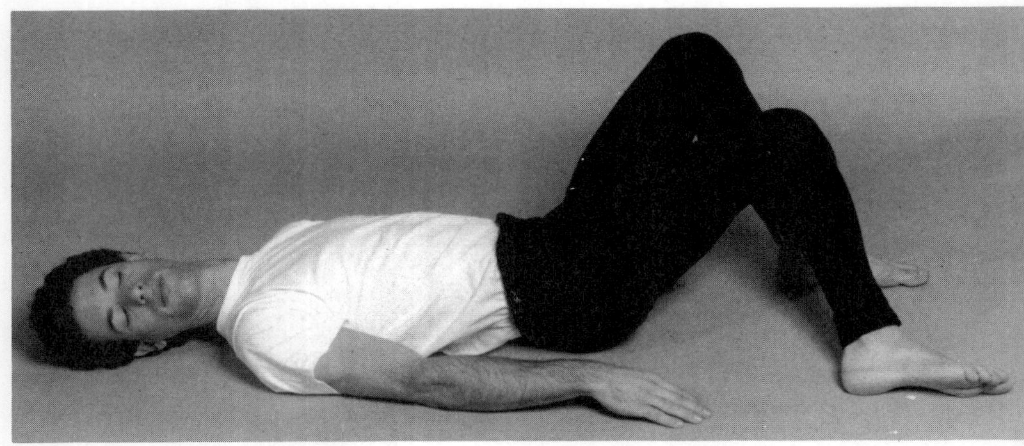

Figure #22.

eyes will be looking out of the left edges of your eye sockets. Gently return to the "neutral" position.

After you repeat this movement several times to become familiar with it, I suggest you also synchronize your breathing as follows: While you let the knee lean and the head roll, slightly part the lips and gently exhale. While you return to the "neutral" position quietly inhale through the nose.

Repeat the movement eight to ten times. Straighten the legs, breathe freely, and reflect on how your body and your mind feel.

11. **Assume the "neutral" position. This time let the right knee slowly and gently lean to the right. Press the left foot softly to the floor. The left hip will come up off the floor slightly. Return to "neutral." Repeat this movement eight to ten times. First you will feel the movement from the pelvis; with repetition you will feel**

the lengthening of the rib cage, shoulder and neck.

12. Straighten the legs, Close your eyes, and try to see on your imaginary screen dark . . . darker . . . darkest . . . black velvet. When you are very tense, it is difficult to visualize only a very dark, black screen. All kinds of flashy colors interfere. Ignore them. With practice, the tension will go away and the flashy spots will disappear.

13. Now let your thoughts concentrate on your breathing. Breathe through the nose—as quietly as possible. Inhale for six counts; then exhale for six counts. Repeat for six breaths.

14. Bend your knees and assume the "neutral" position. Again, add the rolling movement of the head to the leaning movement of the knees. This time lean

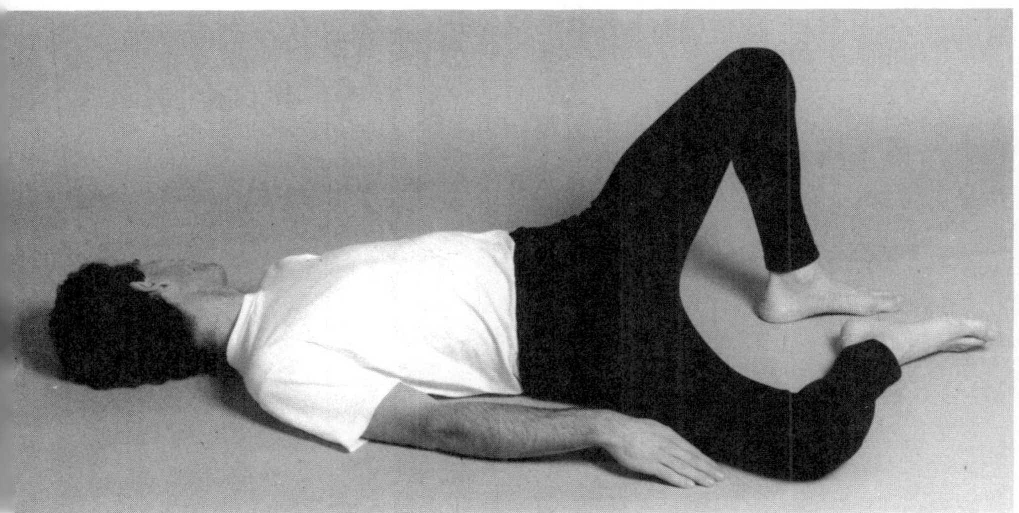

Figure #23.

the right knee to the right and roll the head to the right; then return both head and knee to "neutral." Repeat the movement eight to ten times and then rest.

15   Now, while the knee does the same movement of slowly leaning to the right, the head rolls to the left. See Figure #23. Return to "neutral." Repeat eight to ten times, then stretch the legs and rest.

16.   From the "neutral" position, continue the sequence of dropping the right knee to the right while turning the head to the left, but this time keep the eyes fixed on a point on the ceiling. See Figure #24. Return to "neutral." Repeat eight to ten times. Rest.

Note: although you are repeating the same movements over and over, try to think of each repetition as a new experience. Be aware of how you feel with each repetition, and of the improvement that you feel with each movement.

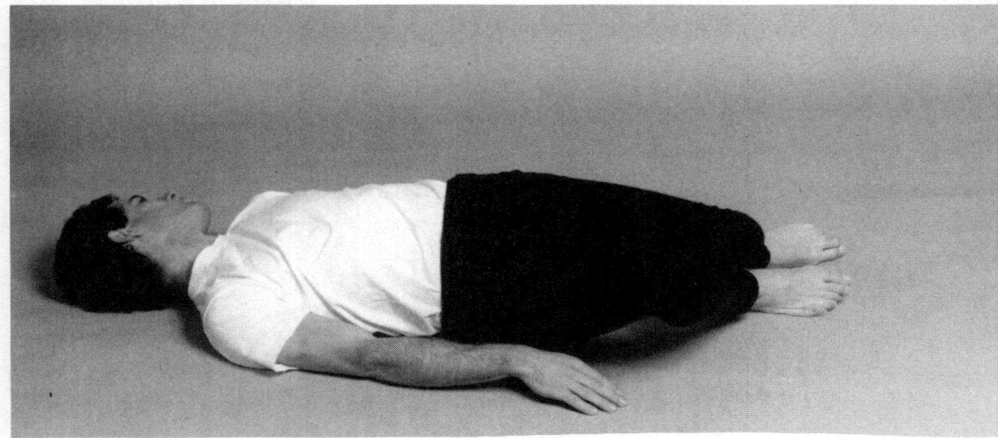

Figure #24.

17. Again, from the "neutral" position, let the right knee fall alternately from side to side, simultaneously rolling the head in the opposite direction while the eyes are fixed on a point on the ceiling. Continue this movement from side to side in a very gentle, easy manner, as if you are in a trance, for at least ten times. Then extend your legs and rest.

18. With your legs extended, inhale through the nose, imagining that you draw the air into the lower part of the abdomen and allowing it to expand as you do so. Now, while holding your breath and not forcing, contract your abdomen by pressing it toward your spine, toward the floor. The air in your lungs will move into the upper part of your chest which will now expand. DO NOT force it! Then relax the abdomen and the air will move into the lowest part of the lungs and the abdomen will expand once again. Part your lips and gently exhale as long as it is very comfortable.

Rest again for a few moments and notice if your body lies flatter, and makes better contact with the floor. Breathe deeply and notice how much more deeply you are breathing. Feel totally relaxed and calm.

19. Assume the "neutral" position once again. Interlace your fingers and place your hands behind your head at the base of your skull. Your head should be resting on your palms. Lift your head one

to two inches from the floor. Have the feeling that someone is pulling the hair at the top of your head away from you, lengthening the nape of your neck. Then, with your head supported by your hands, bring your chin towards your chest. Your forearms are parallel; elbows pointing forward.

Slowly, gently, return the head to the floor while you open the elbows. Breathe out when you bring the chin towards the chest and inhale while you return the head to the floor. With every new movement sense the beginning of it as it starts from lower and lower on the spine. Imagine the nape starts between the shoulder blades; after 7-8 repetitions you will feel the movement starting from the pelvis. Rest, hands along the body, palms down, extend the legs. With your legs extended, roll your head, keeping it on the floor, from side to side. Keep your eyes open, looking from side to side where your head is facing. Sense the increased freedom in your neck.

20. Return to "neutral." Interlace the fingers, place the hands at the base of the back of the head as before and lift the head towards the chest, bringing the elbows parallel. Simultaneously bring your knees toward your elbows. See Figure #25. Feel the back muscles lengthen and you will notice how any lower back pain will go away. Return to "neutral," keeping the hands to the head while

allowing the elbows to open to the sides. Then repeat this curling of the spine movement for six to eight times. However, if you should experience any back pain, avoid this movement.

Lie quietly for a few seconds. Concentrate on your exhalations. With each exhalation let your body weight sag more and more into the floor. Let it go. Let all your muscles relax, let all your thoughts drift away. Your attention is devoted only to your breathing. Roll your head on the floor from side to side; enjoy the freedom you feel in your neck, in your whole body—legs, hip, pelvis. Roll on

63

the side and slowly get up. Avoid any sudden movement.

For my vanity and your encouragement look in a mirror. Be aware of your posture, one eye may be brighter, one half of the face may be more relaxed, wrinkles under the eyes may have disappeared, one shoulder may be lower. Walk about the room and feel the quality of your movement. Although you have worked mostly one side of the body, in a few moments the wisdom of your body and mind will communicate to the whole body. Next time you should practice these exercises with the left leg. You can practice every day; you should do these exercises at least twice a week.

There is a famous Chinese proverb: When I hear . . . I forget. When I see . . . I remember. Only when I do . . . I understand. Only by doing will you understand—and feel!—the rewards.

TO SLEEP OR NOT TO SLEEP

"The sleep is the balm of her mind!!. . . . Shakespeare

To sleep . . . or not to sleep? Einstein slept ten hours a night. For Edison, two hours were enough. And Kafka, Van Gogh, and Proust all suffered from insomnia.

The average person spends a third of his or her life sleeping, or trying to! Some people have difficulty falling asleep; others fall asleep quickly but wake up in the middle of the night, worrying about yesterday or contemplating tomorrow.

I recommend the following exercises for combatting insomnia:

SLEEP . . . SLEEP . . . SLEEP

1. Just before lying down, sit on the edge of your bed and check your breathing. With your fingertips, locate the two small holes on both sides of your upper neck—just below the head bones. See Figure #26. Press and massage these spots in a circular motion for 8 counts. Then release. Repeat this 3 times. Slowly move your fingers inch by inch. Go underneath the skull bones from the upper neck and stop when you are about one inch away from your ears.

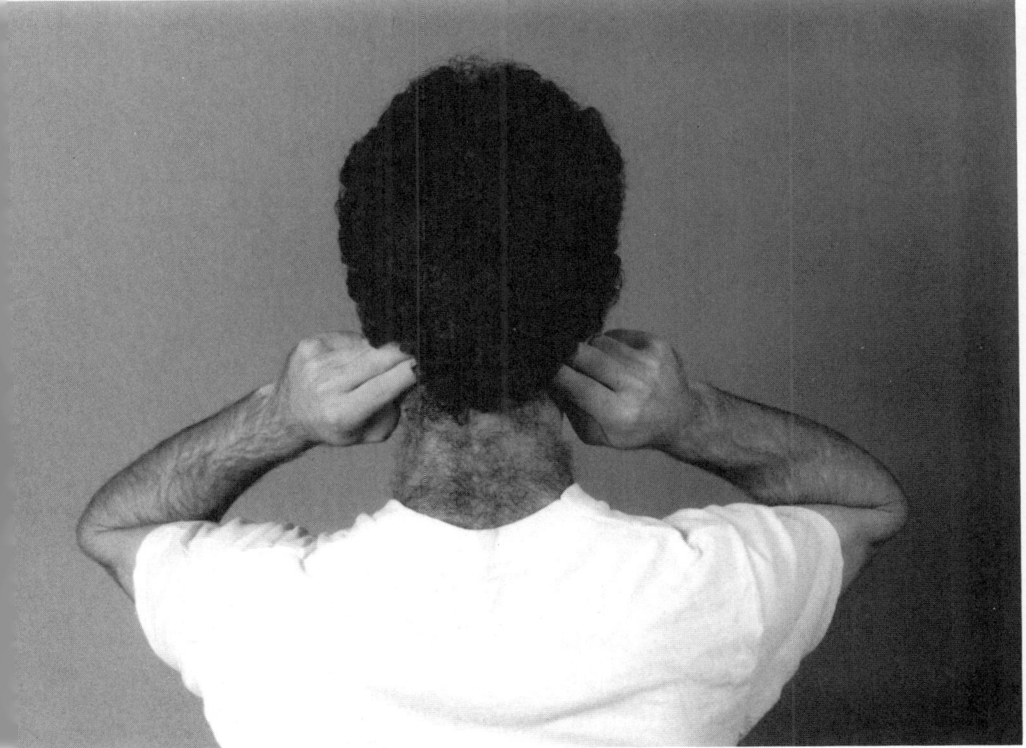

Figure #26.

After you have repeated this exercise 6-8 times, check your breathing. You will notice great improvement in your nasal breathing, an essential ingredient for ensuring sleep and preventing snoring.

2.   **The next treatment is the most powerful tool you can use to relax and to help you get a full night's sleep. It is a "modified" Feldenkrais lesson:**

Lie in bed on your back. Close your eyes and imagine you are seeing a screen of black. It is very dark and keeps getting darker darker . . . darker . . . darker. Then rest.

A. Leave your eyes in the resting position in the middle of the eye socket. Keeping your eyes closed, move the right eye—slowly, easily—toward your right temple. Then slowly bring it back to the center resting position. Do not pass the center. Repeat this eye movement to the right and back to the center 8 times. Breathe out when you move the eye to the right and breathe in when you return it to the resting position. Your breathing should be silent and should come through your nose. You will notice that your breathing becomes easier and easier. Continue to keep your eyes closed during the entire session.

B. Next, move the right eye to its right and hold it there. The movement will be from the upper right corner to the lower right corner—in a semi-arched pattern. Repeat the arched movements 8 times. Return the eye to the center and rest. Notice how much more relaxed the right side of your face feels.

C. With the eyes closed, move the right eye from the center to the upper right corner and back to the center, then to the lower right corner and back to the center, making small diagonals. After repeating this movement 8 times, bring the eye to the center. Rest and enjoy the relaxed sensation that you feel not only on the right side of the face, but on the right side of your entire body.

D. Now circle your right eye without passing the center. The eye should move up toward the forehead, to the right upper corner, then to the right lower corner, down to the cheek and back to the center. I suggest doing about 5 clockwise circles and 5 counterclockwise circles. Since it is the outside peripheral movement of the eye that relaxes the eye, and since all body parts are influenced by the eyes, please do not pass the center position toward the nose.

Continue to leave your eyes closed, trying to see black, black, black. Is it darker than when you started?

If you are still wide awake, repeat the whole pattern with the left eye.

If you wake up during the night, you may want to try an abbreviated version of this exercise. Just cut the a and c sections, and extend the b and d sections.

3. Tension in the jaw often causes sleepless nights. To relax your jaw and to avoid clenching or grinding your teeth during the night do the following: lie on your back while in bed with your face facing the ceiling. Use a pillow if you wish. Close your eyes. Slowly open your mouth and

exhale. At the same time push your head
a tiny bit backwards. Keeping your eyes
closed, look towards the cheeks. Slowly
close your mouth, breathe in through
your nose and bring your head and eyes
back to the starting position. Repeat 5-6
times, if you are still awake. If your sleep
is disturbed by twitching and jerking legs
or by muscular cramps, the most effective
tool is to contract and release the anus.
(See Chapter One.)

Visualization is another excellent technique that will help you fall asleep.

First prepare yourself by doing one of the previous exercises—massaging under the skull, rubbing your ear lobe and exhaling with your wide open mouth. Now choose a favorite place to visit—a bright sandy beach, a beautiful green park, a fragrant country field, perhaps your dream house. Feel the calmness and the beauty of your special place. Feel secure there. Smell the odors and see the colors. Look around and observe more and more details. Every night go back to your favorite place and add new images. If it is a beach, you might watch the birds feeding at the shoreline. If it is a house, add some soft pillows to the couch. Do everything you possibly can to make your refuge comfortable and inviting. You will fall asleep peacefully. The next night you will look forward to visiting and building your dream land.

In addition to the exercises, there are a variety of other ways to improve your sleep. Take for instance these helpful hints:

Some people like to position their beds so
their heads will be facing north and their legs

south. When Charles Dickens traveled, he always carried a compass so he could locate the north and arrange his bed to benefit from the magnetic energy between the two poles.

Check the temperature of your room. It should always be comfortable for you. Many people find it easier to sleep in a reasonably warm room than in a cold one.

Use 100 percent cotton sheets, pajamas and nightgowns instead of those made from artificial fiber.
Make sure your pillows are filled with pure materials rather than synthetics.

Consider sleeping naked if night clothes restrict your movements.

Try a warm—not hot—relaxing bath or have a glass of milk just before going to bed.

An evening meal of pasta and salad is known to induce sleep.

Do not drink too much coffee, tea or wine before going to sleep.

Whatever you do, don't become obsessed with your insomnia. Try and take a catnap during the day. This will help you extend your energy into the evening.
Remember that the quality of your sleep during the night will influence your work and creativity during the day. Sleep well!

LAST MINUTE ADVICE AND QUICK RECOVERIES

Be committed but not compulsive.
Be determined but not aggressive.
Be powerful but flexible.

Professional success depends on one's flexibility to cope with stress. So many great talents—musicians, singers, dancers—had to give up their careers because they could not cope with stage-fright. Many had to give up because physical problems related to stress prevented them from performing.

In most cases we don't "fall" sick, we "slide" into sickness. Over 70% of health problems are rooted in tension. Although tension can be caused by a traumatic experience most tension is the result of a series of small events which recur frequently and create an accumulated deficit in our emotional balance.

All the fundamental methods which deal with tension have some common basic principles:

1. Under tension we contract our muscles which in turn affect our posture. Chronically contracted muscles produce pain in the neck, shoulders and lower back, weaken the organs, and restrict breathing.
2. The way we breathe affects our well-being. The air we breathe is the most important source of vital energy. Under tension we breathe poorly.
3. The pelvis is a magnet for accumulating tension and sex life suffers. Releasing tension in general and the pelvis in particular,

will improve your sex life. (See chapter
Preventive Treatment)

The wisdom of your body can help you; listen
to it. When you are tired or angry, sighing, yawning,
yelling, screaming are S.O.S. signals for more oxygen.

A deep laugh activates the respiratory muscles. There are clinics where the main treatment is
laughing!

Treatments and therapists, regular exercise
sessions and instructors involve considerable expense.
The goal of this book is to teach you to "do it yourself"
very effectively. But if you have the time and money
don't exclude other methods you are attracted to. Regular exercising, and massage that includes shiatsu, re-
flexology, and accupressure will complement and enhance the benefits of my advice.

If I have repeated and repeated some movements it is because they are basic and I want to emphasize them. The variations are carefully chosen to adapt
to places and times.

If I have still not convinced you how much
posture influences the body, raise your shoulders as
high as you can and breathe in and out. Now lower
the shoulders and breathe in and out. Compare how
restricted your breathing is when your shoulders are
up and how much freer and deeper your breathing is
when your shoulders are down.

To relax and recharge any time, anywhere,
here is the most effective "instant trick" I know. It is a
synthesis of several techniques recommended in this
book:

1. **Press the lowest part of the abdomen to-
    ward the spine while exhaling, and drop**

the chin onto your chest. After a comfortable exhalation—long but not forceful—hold the position, contract the anus and simultaneously swallow, then LET IT GO completely, from the toes to the crown of your head. Some people will feel the need to shake. Do it! Shake your whole body; then rest a few seconds until you recover your uncontrolled breathing. It is a powerful way to relax and recharge. Do this 2 or 3 times, no more. Between each cycle leave time to feel the benefits. You can practice a few times during the day, whether standing or seated. If seated, the legs should be uncrossed and the feet on the floor; if standing the knees should be slightly bent, not over-extended.

2. When you cannot concentrate on your work and feel mentally exhausted, try this for some quick mental energy: Using the knuckles knock the head gently all around the skull—not the face. After about 50-60 seconds stop and be aware of the renewed energy. Your AWARENESS will help to improve the benefits of the exercise.

3. When anxiety starts to engulf you, tap the breast bone—the sternum, not the breast—for a few seconds with the tips of your fingers.

4. The following is an excellent way to release tension and energize the body, but I don't recommend it for anyone who suffers from high blood pressure:

Tense the anus, tense the genitals, close the eyes and tense them, squeeze the mouth into the shape of a child's kiss, raise the shoulders as high as you can tense them, and tense the whole body for a few seconds and RELEASE. . . ! LET IT GO. . . !

Another instant energizer trick also combats jet lag, and can be practiced by everyone.

5. **Take off your shoes and stockings. With bare feet rub the soles of the feet on a carpet. The rougher the carpet the better.**

Some people are inclined to tense up very easily, while others are more resistant; but nobody is "tension proof."

There are many apparently irrelevant small factors which play a big part in building tension. For example, the color of your clothes, the way your shoes fit, lights, particularly the lights where you work. Check to see if you hold your toothbrush, comb, pen, or phone with more than necessary force.

One of the most common sources of tensing the upper body is the way we hold the phone while talking. A great number of people hold the receiver between their neck and shoulder. The neck and the ribcage are the immediate victims.

Not long ago I met a very successful person. It was obvious that tension was eating him up. Glad that he asked me about my work, I promptly advocated the cause, insisting what a fruitful investment it is to spend a few minutes doing something to release tension. Shaking his head he told me he was so incredibly busy, he could not afford even a few minutes during the day or evening. Besides, he assured me, he was fine, fine, fine! A few days later he had a heart attack.

It is up to you to be aware and judge for yourself what helps you and what you enjoy doing. Only by enjoying, will you practice regularly without feeling, "I hate it but I must do it."

The biblical sage, Hillel, used to say . . . "If I am not for myself, who will be for me?" He also used to say: "If not now, when?"

The great advantage of the release of tension methods is that age is never a limit for the benefits.

My sincere hope is that after reading this book you will no longer think about "taking" or "not taking" time to do the exercises. Rather, you will want to give yourself a few moments each day, knowing you are giving yourself the gift of energy and flexibility, the gift of renewed, better-functioning organs, and the gift of an attractive, healthy appearance every day of your life.

P.S.

After I completed the manuscript for this book, I heard of a very efficient healer who is said to cure health problems caused by tension. He was recommended to me by a very respectable orchestral manager who is not particularly inclined to esoteric approaches. So. . . , I went.

The healer combines massage with some mystical words and synchronizes his breathing with the client's rhythm of breathing. He also uses crystals and herbs in ways I could not understand.

After a few sessions, he showed me one of his most successful treatments to combat tiredness and lack of energy. To my great enjoyment, it was an exercise, slightly modified, which you have already encountered in this book. I continue to recommend it for any situation when you feel tired. How many times have you awakened, even after a full night of sleep, still tired, not ready to face the world. Please, with full confidence, include the following exercise in your morning wake-up ritual, and repeat it during the day whenever you are feeling "low."

Standing, seated, or lying down, interlace the fingers and place your hands behind your head at the base of your skull, as in Figure #18. Keeping the spine extended, with the help of your hands, slowly, very slowly, lower your head—chin toward your chest. Open your mouth and exhale, releasing a sigh from all the depths of your being. Keeping the chin toward your chest, inhale with a short sniff through the nose. Continue to keep the head lowered, and repeat the long and relieving exhalation followed by a short—like a sniff—inhalation. Practice the cycle four to six times;

then slowly, very slowly, bring the head back up and release your hands.

Whenever you feel "low" do not let yourself sink lower with self-pity; have the will-power to do something to change your outlook. Here is a slightly modified Biblical meditation: God, help me to accept what I cannot change, and to change what I can.

Bibliography

Alon, Ruthy. *Mindful Spontaneity—Lessons in the F. Method.* Avery Publishing Group, New York, 1990.

Barlow, Wilfred, Ed. *More Talk of Alexander: Aspects of the Alexander Principle.* Victor Gollancz, Ltd., London, 1978.

Benson, Herbert, M.D. *The Relaxation Response.* Avon Books, New York, 1975.

————*Beyond the Relaxation Response.* Berkeley Books, New York, 1985.

Byles, Marie Beuzeville. *Stand Straight Without Strain—The Method and Original Exercises by Matthias Alexander.* L. N. Fowler & Co. Essex, 1978.

Feldenkrais, Moshe. *Body & Mature Behaviour.* Alef Publisher, Ltd., Tel Aviv. 1949.

————. *The Potent Self.* Harper & Row, New York, 1985.

————. *Awareness Through Movement.* Harper & Row, New York, 1972.

————. *The Master Moves.* Meta Publications, California, 1984.

Grindea, Carola, Ed. *Tensions in the Performance of Music.* Pro/Am Music Resources, White Plains, 1987.

Hanna, Thomas. *The Body of Life.* Alfred A. Knopf, New York, 1980.

Houston, Jean. *The Possible Human.* J.P. Tarcher, Inc. Los Angeles, 1982.

Kushi, Michio. *The Book of Do-In.* Japan Publications, 1979.

Leibowitz, Judith and Connington, Bill. *The Alexander Technique.* Harper & Row, New York, 1990.

Linklater, Kristin. *Freeing the Natural Voice.* Drama Book Publishers, New York, 1976.

Loehr, Dr. James and Migdow, Dr. Jeffrey. *Take a Deep Breath.* Villard Books, New York, 1986.

Lowen, Alexander, M.D. *Bioenergetics.* Penguin Books. London, 1976.

Masters, Robert and Houston, Jean. *Listening to the Body.* Delacorte Press, New York, 1978.

Pearls, Frederick, Hefferline, Ralph F., and Goodman, Pam. *Gestalt Therapy.* Bantan Books, New York, 1977.

Rolf, Ida. *Ida Rolf Talks About Rolfing and Physical Reality.* Harper & Row, New York, 1978.

Russel, Peter. *The Brain Book.* E. P. Dutton, New York, 1979.

Selye, Hans, M.D. *The Stress of Life.* McGraw Hill Book Co., New York, 1956.

————— *Stress without Distress.* New American Library, New York, 1975.

Speads, Carola. *Breathing: The ABC's.* Harper & Row, New York, 1978.

Stroebel, Charles F., M.D. *Q R: The Quieting Reflex.* Berkeley Books, New York, 1983.

Woolfolk, Robert and Lehrer, Paul, Eds. *Principles and Practice of Stress Management.* The Guildford Press, New York & London, 1984.